Little Poems
Kathleen Ossip

VERVE
POETRY PRESS
BIRMINGHAM

PUBLISHED BY VERVE POETRY PRESS
https://vervepoetrypress.com
mail@vervepoetrypress.com

All rights reserved
© 2022 Kathleen Ossip

The right of Kathleen Ossip to be identified as author of this work has been asserted in accordance with section 77 of the Copyright, Designs and Patents Act 1988.

No part of this work may be reproduced, stored or transmitted in any form or by any means, graphic, electronic, recorded or mechanical, without the prior written permission of the publisher.

FIRST PUBLISHED SEP 2022

Printed and bound in the UK by Imprint Digital, Exeter

ISBN: 978-1-913917-16-6

CONTENTS

Stones	6
Living Room	7
The Problem of Hope	8
Weigela	13
Cicadas	14
Theology	15
A Collection	16
A Tragedy	17
Donald Trump Pines for Love	18
Snow Song	19
On First Reading Susan Wheeler	20
On First Meeting Roddy Lumsden	21
Art	22
The Facts	23
Lines Written While Crying	25
Places I Have Lived	26
Marriage	27
Puzzle Piece	28
Henry Hudson	29
Words on a Monument	30
Van Gogh, *The Sower*	31
From the Sixth Floor	32
Final	33

Acknowledgements

In memory
Roddy Lumsden

Little Poems

Stones

A group of women I'm a part of had a falling out, or falling apart, about whether stones and rocks are alive. One woman passionately argued that they were. Others counter-argued with biological facts like breath, growth, movement, reproduction. So passionate was the woman who believed stones were alive that she left the group in anger. On leaving, she told us that her beliefs were religious and based on Native American traditions that everything on earth is alive. There is no hierarchy of being.

Today, walking on the obsolete aqueduct, I met all kinds of rocks and stones. Some were embedded into the dry soil, polished by footsteps, revealing only their flat satin faces. Others were more petite, round, loose, and whimsical. Some were tiny: Where does gravel end and pebble begin? Their colors and shapes were various. All seemed interesting and individual. Each completely filled the outlines of its spirit.

I've noticed that debates rarely come to any conclusion. Instead, they make the outlines of division more definite and fixed. However, they are perhaps inescapable pitfalls of being alive, or at least being human. I can imagine an existence where semantic arguments (all arguments are semantic) didn't occupy such a central irritating spot, where the work of soothing others was paramount. I need all the friends I can get, happy to count stones among them.

Living Room

Square of sun engraved on the goldtone wall.
Within, shadow of thornbranch.

The lengthened leaves agitate:
constrained hands flapping.

The leafshadows twist like victims.
They aren't victims.

I have a body, not shown here.

You have a body and may
see such things one day.

The Problem of Hope

in memory John Ashbery

1.

It stumps, the meagerness of hope,
which can never shout with
as full a throat as its enemies.

You discover you don't want to hope,
and there's absolutely no reason to.
All hope is latent,

the way all cats are opiated—
absurdly.
All hope is manic,

like a fastfood chain
trying desperately hard
to be good for you too.

Yet I believe
in the secret small work of hope.

2.

Who made hope forlorn anyway?
The nasty paradox of hope,
that it switches on just when, necessarily,

it can't achieve its end.
If you ever were hopeful,
you'll be hopeful again

like the woman
who joined the search party
looking for her

and thus was found.
As a new apartment doesn't feel like home
until you've been out all day

and come back at night,
hope settles in once you recognize
its current usefulness,

its roof.

3.

Hope deferred
makes the heart sick,
but a longing fulfilled is a tree of life.

4.

When I think of
the old masters, whose hopes,
like shingles on a house,

have slipped out of notch,

fifty times I hope
for every cent
they never spent.

5.

Years start dying
and the man with hair the color
of dandelion fuzz

prepares to conclude
his cave-like jest.
He predicted much,

deduced not at all.
Imagine you have hope—
why would you reject

the ideas he prodigally included?
He tenders social hope,
evocations of pleasure

and solitude and how steadily
we now and then believe.
Petals drop through the fog

with abandon.
Fifty times you hope.
May your troubles be appeased.

Weigela

The weigela does its dusty thing...
John Ashbery

The light is tight.
The dust is kind.
The tight makes all
the blossoms bright
and spares the mind
(pinkly they fall)
from being right.

Cicadas

We admit we're ridiculous.
That droning noise
sheer attention-
seeking. We wiggle
our tymbals
and hope for the best.
We're not unique
in all the universe.
We shudder with others
and mean it.

Theology

The bronze Buddha and his companion the brass cat
are so small, how could they pose a danger to anyone?

The cat turns its face to the corner.
The Buddha looks right at us, but smilingly.

Don't worry. They are gentle as two pats of butter.

A Collection

A scarlet tin star bursts its compartment
in the display case.

One Buddha coexists
with a brass Egyptian cat.

Another is dwarfed by a gilt-capped test tube
which might be a soul-body metaphor.

No collection can keep honest
without a pocketwatch.

How flexibly the several thick white hairs
lean in *their* compartment.

From the collector's head
or a cat's face? An ivory skull,

an ivory skull, an ivory skull, an ivory skull—
they'd make nice earrings.

A tanned rose, once fresh.
Oh, there are *two* pocketwatches.

A possible third bends its sheen
away from the curious and backs into the gloom.

A Tragedy

You say there's too little of earth, that you want more?
A dead deer named Germany
to be apportioned like Germany?
A life more
consequential than it meant to be?

Did we have mouths?
Did we listen to the experts?
Did we chant in the—what was it—forest?

We wanted. Then they changed the penalty.
Disappearance is a shy gift,
an emotion.
Color: lavender-gray.

We thought want a form of love.
Oh we made tragedy sleet
high and nationwide.

Donald Trump Pines for Love

Eyes again answered you not.
Something, the so-silver light, cleared and
you sniffled too.
You the soft. You bowed
then softly could see.

Goodbye, name.
Your air was before.

What could ever stamp out your losses?
Waving hair is never of she.
Oh, choose to if only, choose seeking.
Your whole biography cramps down as
The One appears, calls, calls:

Not I— I— I—

Snow Song

Clouds make a meaning of snow.
Snow is the meaning of clouds.
The tune of the snow is a color.
The history of snow's in the stiffening gutter.

Headlights mock the snow (or vice versa).
The end of the snow is morning.
The sunlight rings the bell of snow.
Snow is dread rewarded.

The cliché of snow is quiet.
The intelligence of snow is private.
The truth of the snow is scientific.
The joke of the snow curls in my mitten.

On First Reading Susan Wheeler

57th Street, c. 1995

In Coliseum Books, the calendars
imply DECEMBER. Answers I have none,
or feeble. And how could questions be sources
of pleasure or of profit? Her answers flick:
blue or *29* or *candlebright*.
December windows. Snowflakes spit like candles.
Cold, and books on shelves that make me cold.
All around, on shelves, final lines shrivel,
dead filaments in a lightbulb. Who can stop
without subtracting? Only, it seems, she.

It was "What Memory Reveals" and I
lived near Columbus Avenue at the time.
How sickening that fallow orange juice in
all the most delicious ways! It said:
You're responsible for your own zoo.
I stretched toward it, the zoo, which had been alien,
like a train journey when a stranger buys you an ice cream,
or like the corner of 12th and Sixth, or like
her individual & traditional talent,
which stays a stranger, but lights up with enthusiasm;
which stays a stranger, but lights up—lights up—lights.

On First Meeting Roddy Lumsden

Ear Inn, Spring Street
January 19, 2002

Light: supreme optical clarity, quick-dry, scratch-resistant.
Clouds: feather-pregnant, groaning, insistent.

Exterior: A puzzle, one continuous Olde New Yorke alley.
I did not know you. You did not know me.

Interior: You. Me. Cheap-ish beer. Warm-ish tea. Sonnets.
Yours: My Dark Side, My Pain. Mine: My Best Self, My Luvox.

The possessive a tack, pinning 14 lines to the Beat wall.
Yours: Thick and celtic, crafty. 14 lines tacked outside the confessional.

We hid the secret we were too shy to give:
It's only part of what I do, the other part is live.

Confess! Confess! But poets don't list sins.
Dreams at night never alter where the morning begins.

Exit and scene: New friends, happy. And un-.
Words I didn't dream to say: *Goodbye! Next year in London!*

Art

With brave reserve, the painter regards a floor lamp, a plum, and a pool stick and reacts. The painting comes out in

flamboyant, fearful drag. The Rezillos sound from the speaker. As in Judaism, the oil lasts far longer than possible.

A painting makes its own luck.

The Facts

The facts sit in an ordinary room. They resemble people: stubborn and without imagination.

The facts begin to chatter: Better days coming, better days coming. They arrange themselves in the shape of a lie.

They're cheating: they only work in the past tense.

They fake objectivity. They decide unanimously.

For example, what do you call that white pointed cylinder generated by the roof on freezing days?

Hang-ice? I say.

Facts say wrong.

The facts await their moment.

In my early years, I didn't think meadows came at a cost. There are no turnstiles or box offices at the edges of a meadow.

The facts told me different. They used the word *property*. And I resented them!

Handle them: they have an activating feel.

The facts dispose like people.

They can mute us. And we can mute them.

Lines Written While Crying

Thoughts: don't listen to them!
These influences, out of all available influences,

too scant to feed,
too cheerless for belief.

So watch me attack and dethrone God,
no longer pretending

this or that central question.
Pileated woodpecker, two crinkled women, a dying mall

emerge into my godless world,
original and beautiful. Beautiful and surprising!

But in terms of weather,
what is wild that doesn't impossibly get old?

Places I Have Lived

Only the just
sleep the sleep of the just.

Only the unjust
know how to punish.

Someone's broken heart
lives in the ruined barn

in Ohio, North America,
on planet Earth.

The unjust break my heart,
the day takes breath.

How will I
ever say what I want to say.

Marriage

So much for the fighting
                         and the sex,
I want to be alone
with you in the next room.

Puzzle Piece

She scrapes at first
against the edge
of her neighbor.
Her color is
tested. If right
she is swallowed
by her role in
the big picture.
If wrong she is
flipped onto a
breath-held pile of
postponements, pitched
aside for her
outlandish shape.
If the last, she
endures the lot
of the fetish:
princess for a
centisecond,
then ignored once
completion is
had. Small wonder
that she sometimes
craftily finds
another box,
sparing herself
the losing face
of fitting in.

Henry Hudson

Wood is a masculine substance.
Witness the Arts and Crafts movement,
the men at the helm of it.
Witness, for that matter, this room:
Oak floor, oak walls, oaken ceiling.
The air conditioning grate: ersatz oak.
The slats of the ceiling fan oak veneer.
The table I write on, particle board
with no pretense to oak, oak's sad cousin.
And the craftsman-style light fixtures, triangles,
right angles, dreamed up in the minds of geometers.
What does geometry illuminate?
I'm the sad cousin of a mind.

The Arts and Crafts men were reacting
against Victorian furbelows, the ornamented empire,
or, as they might have said, civilization.
Still, this room is only the sad cousin of nature.
It has its smoke alarm, its watercooler,
its green exit sign (a threat, not an invitation),
its lectern, its monumental fireplace of unpolished granite,
its coffeemaker. Out the west-facing window
I can see, flat and small as a playing card,
the platinum slice of river, and beyond,
the wiry cliffs of the Palisades. *The sun is setting*,
pronounces Henry Hudson, eternally facing west,
bobbling on the deck of the *Halve Maen*.

Words on a Monument

We do not
regret our time
though our
motives smudged
and the
atmosphere

plummets.

We are
only a minor
aftereffect
of the Greeks,

inexplicably
un
gone.

Van Gogh, *The Sower*

Sometimes it comes to me like a punch in the face how deluded I've been my entire life.

The song lyrics, the movies. The three-act arcs.

I'm supposed to see the humble work ethic of the man sowing.

The setting sun makes a halo for him. What a contrast to his furtive stance, thief's vestments.

The seeds clearly point to a brighter future.

Dear VVG,
A poem is what happens in the abyss between spectacle and experience

as you know.

I like the scythe-shaped things coming off the tree because I don't know why you put them there.

From the Sixth Floor

The church spire's a grandmother, crafted, hoping.
The chimney's a grandfather, tense and solid.
The slate roof's a mother, spread out and open.
The mansard a father, blind, helmeted.
The gray trees are children, their fingers velveted.
The cold leaves their ideas, broken and broken.

Final

My body has gone.
It doesn't need me anymore.

It reminds me of myself,
saying prayers,

sharing old stories.
We are deep in something, with this sharing.

The wave approaches,
turns, swells.

It might cleanse the choices
we are trying to make right.

I'm re-conceiving everything I knew:
the history of upper New York State,

arsenal town, mill, factory, dock.
It reminds me of my body, gone but real.

We are deep in something.
We all have it so hard right now.

Let me welcome you
to the republic of smiles.

Let me be your founding mother.
Lay your fever on my shoulder.

—What do you feel like eating, dear?
—Nothing really, I just ate.

I'm not offended.
It's a relief to me too.

How do you re-conceive a history?
Can kindness buy peace?

Does the moon still talk to me?
Only every night.

ACKNOWLEDGEMENTS

Thank you to the editors of these journals, which first published some of the poems:

Bennington Review, On the Seawall, Ladowich, The New Statesman, The Paris Review, Oxford Poetry, The Journal, Sewanee Review, Court Green, Poetry London, New York Review of Books

Boundless gratitude to Kristina Andersson Bicher and Spencer Short, who had patience with the poems and improved them.

Italicized lines in "The Problem of Hope" are from Proverbs 13:12.

"Donald Trump Pines for Love" began as a cutup of Rita Dove's "Happenstance."

The final line of the chapbook appears in an episode of *Mad Men*.

ABOUT VERVE POETRY PRESS

Verve Poetry Press is a quite new and already award-winning press that focussed initially on meeting a local need in Birmingham - a need for the vibrant poetry scene here in Brum to find a way to present itself to the poetry world via publication. Co-founded by Stuart Bartholomew and Amerah Saleh, it now publishes poets from all corners of the UK and beyond - poets that speak to the city's varied and energetic qualities and will contribute to its many poetic stories.

Added to this is a colourful pamphlet series, many featuring poets who have performed at our sister festival - and a poetry show series which captures the magic of longer poetry performance pieces by festival alumni such as Polarbear, Matt Abbott and Imogen Stirling.

The press has been voted Most Innovative Publisher at the Saboteur Awards, and has won the Publisher's Award for Poetry Pamphlets at the Michael Marks Awards.

Like the festival, we strive to think about poetry in inclusive ways and embrace the multiplicity of approaches towards this glorious art.

https://vervepoetrypress.com
@VervePoetryPres
mail@vervepoetrypress.com